What Happens in Fall?

Pumpkins in Fall

by Mari Schuh

Bullfrog Books

Ideas for Parents and Teachers

Bullfrog Books let children practice reading informational text at the earliest reading levels. Repetition, familiar words, and photo labels support early readers.

Before Reading

• Discuss the cover photo. What does it tell them?

• Look at the picture glossary together. Read and discuss the words.

Read the Book

• "Walk" through the book and look at the photos. Let the child ask questions. Point out the photo labels.

• Read the book to the child, or have him or her read independently.

After Reading

• Prompt the child to think more. Ask: Where do you see pumpkins in the fall? What do they look like?

Bullfrog Books are published by Jump!
5357 Penn Avenue South
Minneapolis, MN 55419
www.jumplibrary.com

Library of Congress Cataloging-in-Publication Data

Schuh, Mari C., 1975-
 Pumpkins in fall / by Mari Schuh.
   p. cm. — (Bullfrog books. What happens in fall?)
 Summary: "Visit a pumpkin patch and learn how pumpkins grow and how they are made into jack-o-lanterns. Color photos and easy-to-read text tell kids about this favorite symbol of the fall season"—Provided by publisher.
 Audience: 005.
 Audience: K to grade 3.
 Includes bibliographical references and index.
 ISBN 978-1-62031-060-1 (hardcover: alk. paper)
 ISBN 978-1-62031-476-0 (paperback)
 ISBN 978-1-62496-078-9 (ebook)
1. Pumpkin—Juvenile literature.
2. Pumpkin—Harvesting—Juvenile literature.
3. Autumn—Juvenile literature. I. Title.
 SB347.S36 2014
 635'.62—dc23
                                    2013001952

Series Editor: Rebecca Glaser
Series Designer: Ellen Huber
Book Designer: Heather Dreisbach
Photo Researcher: Heather Dreisbach

Photo Credits: Dreamstime, 3, 5, 21, 23bl; Shutterstock, cover, 1, 6–7, 8, 9, 10, 13, 15, 17, 18, 19, 20, 22 main, 22 insert, 23tr, 23mr, 23br, 23tl, 23ml, 24; Superstock, 4, 12, 16.

Printed in the United States of America at Corporate Graphics in North Mankato, Minnesota.

Dedicated to Addison Caruso of Kenosha, Wisconsin. — Mari Schuh

Table of Contents

Let's Pick a Pumpkin

It is fall.

Let's go to the pumpkin patch.

All summer, the pumpkins grow.

In fall, they are ripe.

Do you see the vines?

Pumpkins grow
on long vines.

stem

Do you see the stem?
It is short and thick.

The patch is full
of pumpkins.

Mei picks a big one.

Kate picks a
small one.

Look!

Bill sees a white pumpkin.

It is called an albino.

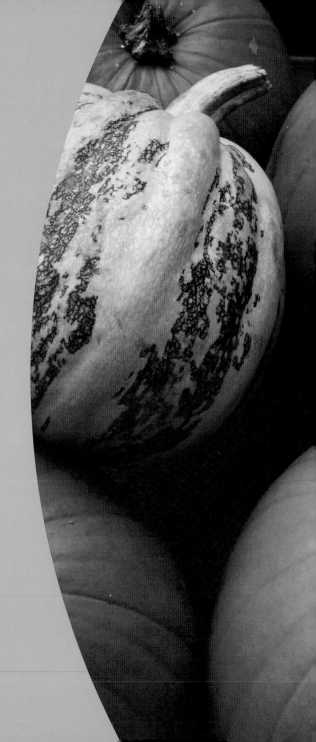

Halloween will be here soon.

Let's carve our pumpkins.

First, Mom cuts
off the top.

Mike scoops out
the seeds.

Then Dad carves
a face.

Andy puts a candle inside.

Now it's a jack-o'-lantern. Boo!

Parts of a Pumpkin

stem
The part of the pumpkin that attaches to the vine.

pulp
The orange inside of a pumpkin that people cook.

rind
The outer skin of a pumpkin.

seeds
The small parts that can grow more pumpkins.

Picture Glossary

carve
To make by cutting.

pumpkin patch
An area of land where lots of pumpkins grow.

Halloween
A holiday that children celebrate by wearing costumes and asking for treats.

ripe
Fully grown and ready to be picked.

jack-o'-lantern
A pumpkin with a carved face and a candle inside.

vine
A plant with a long, winding stem.

Index

To Learn More

Learning more is as easy as 1, 2, 3.

1) Go to www.factsurfer.com

2) Enter "pumpkins" into the search box.

3) Click the "Surf" button to see a list of websites.

With factsurfer.com, finding more information is just a click away.